The Library of
Political Assassinations

The Assassination of
Abraham Lincoln

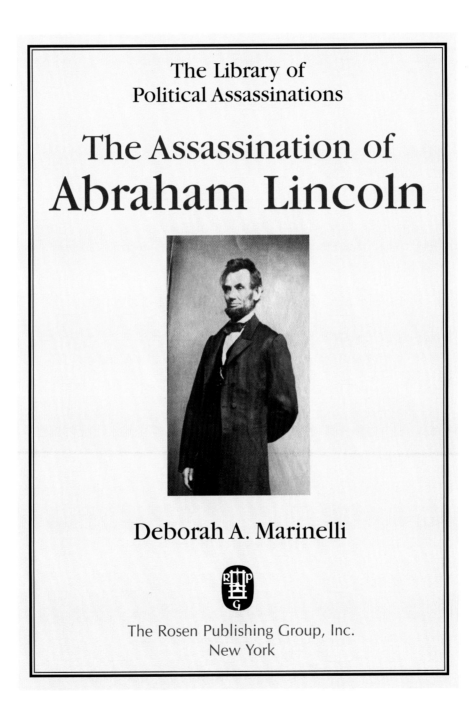

Deborah A. Marinelli

The Rosen Publishing Group, Inc.
New York

*For Larry, Christian, Rachel, and Jim
And my thanks to Annie Sommers*

Published in 2002 by The Rosen Publishing Group, Inc.
29 East 21st Street, New York, NY 10010

Library of Congress Cataloging-in-Publication Data

Marinelli, Deborah A.
The assassination of Abraham Lincoln / Deborah A. Marinelli. —
1st ed.
p. cm. — (The library of political assassinations)
Summary: Discusses the lives of Abraham Lincoln and John Wilkes
Booth, the political reasons for, and details of, the assassination
plan, and Lincoln's legacy.
ISBN 0-8239-3539-6 (lib. bdg.)
1. Lincoln, Abraham, 1809-1865—Assassination—Juvenile literature.
[1. Lincoln, Abraham, 1809-1865—Assassination. 2. Booth, John
Wilkes, 1838-1865. 3. Assassins. 4. United States—History—Civil
War, 1861-1865.] I. Title. II. Series.
E457.5.M24 2001
973.7'092–dc21
[B]

2001002762

Manufactured in the United States of America

(Previous page) Abraham Lincoln, the sixteenth president of
the United States and the first to be assassinated

Contents

The statue of Abraham Lincoln at the Lincoln Memorial is
nineteen feet high and was designed by American sculptor
Daniel Chester French. During the 1960s, African Americans
often gathered at the memorial demanding equal rights.

Introduction

Abraham Lincoln, the sixteenth president of the United States, is remembered as a martyr and hero who freed the slaves and ended the American Civil War. The majestic Lincoln Memorial in Washington, D.C., commemorates his achievements.

In his own day, however, Lincoln was not so highly regarded. He was self-taught, and though he passed the Illinois Bar to become a successful lawyer, he had only one year of formal education. Lincoln always considered this a handicap, but his love of reading and his capacity for study and deep thought made up for his missed opportunity to attend regular classes. Lincoln refused to clutter his mind with anything less than the greatest books, so his ideas were shaped by some of the most important writers and thinkers of history, such as Socrates and Shakespeare. Sometimes Lincoln was plagued with black moods, probably a result of losing his mother at the age of nine. Though he had a great sense of humor, throughout his life he suffered from spells of depression, particularly when, as president, he received news of the deaths of young soldiers at the front.

This flag was flown to show support for Lincoln during his campaign for a second term as president of the United States.

Lincoln spoke honestly and plainly, but he had none of the social polish of the other men who served in his cabinet. Because of this, these officials often felt superior to Lincoln. Many men and women idcalized him, however, as someone from their own background who had thrust himself into the top rungs of national leadership by working hard.

Lincoln ran for president on the Republican ticket. In those days, this carried little prestige and was, in fact, seen as another strike against him. The Republican Party was quite young and inexperienced, having first loosely organized in 1854, less than six years before Lincoln's first run for the White House. However, under the president's firm direction, it quickly grew in influence.

An Embattled President

The American Civil War lasted from 1861 to 1865. Any war is tragic, but the American Civil War was doubly so, for it divided the country between North and South.

The war set brother against brother, and cousin against cousin. Although there were complex economic reasons for this bloody quarrel—the Northern states were mostly industrial, the Southern states were mostly agricultural, and their key interests were opposed to one another—the American Civil War is primarily remembered as when President Lincoln issued the Emancipation Proclamation in 1863.

Union commander George B. McClellan (with his hand on the stump) ignored Lincoln's ideas about the Union's military campaigns and strategies.

Lincoln's family suffered throughout the war because his wife Mary's brothers fought for the Confederacy while Lincoln was commander in chief of the Union forces. This placed the president in the position of having to support military campaigns that could wound or even kill his wife's family. This was not his only sorrow.

Trouble in the Chain of Command

As Lincoln's knowledge of military and government operations increased, men who were supposed to be his loyal advisers were often disrespectful. Some refused to take his orders. Some of his most important advisers, and a number of foreign ambassadors, thought of Lincoln as a bumbling backwoodsman. General George B. McClellan turned a deaf ear to Lincoln's thoughts on the Union's military campaign, and Secretary of State William Seward believed that he was wiser than the president when it came to foreign affairs. McClellan was eventually fired, and Seward was forced to adjust his attitude, but it was a rough beginning for Lincoln, who had only a few men around him whom he could trust.

A Backwoodsman Prevails

Despite the contempt of those he needed in his corner, Lincoln surprised his critics and became one of the greatest presidents of all time. The fact that he was cut down at his most triumphant moment made his legend more poignant. Although many criticized Lincoln during his lifetime, few dared to speak ill of him after his tragic and unexpected death. Unfortunately, only when the president was gone did the country and Lincoln's own staff fully realize the skill and courage it had taken for him to press on with a dangerous military campaign and the freeing of the slaves. Only then, as his own secretary of war, Edwin McMasters Stanton, said, did the murdered head-of-state become "one with the Ages."

Images of Lincoln chopping wood contributed to his mystique as a frontiersman. (Incidentally, he was the inspiration for Lincoln Logs, the popular children's toys.)

Chapter

The Night Lincoln Was Shot

On April 14, 1865, President Lincoln had just started his second term. He was utterly exhausted and looked at least a decade older than his fifty-six years. Photographs taken then show him as an old, wizened man. The war had robbed the lives of 600,000 young soldiers, and these casualties had taken a huge toll on Lincoln. His personal life offered little comfort. By the last years of his first term, his marriage to Mary Todd Lincoln was greatly strained by the deaths of their young sons Eddie and Willie.

Mary Todd Lincoln

Lincoln had married the pretty and energetic Mary Todd in 1842. Though Mary had always led a life of privilege, the two had much in common: Both had lost their mothers when they were young, and both were intensely interested in politics. Though the Lincolns loved each other very much, the fact that they both suffered from depression complicated their lives.

As first lady, Mary spent far more money than the president made and often quarreled with their friends. Mary's actions were unpredictable and were sometimes criticized as peculiar; she was ridiculed for holding séances in the White House in an attempt to contact her dead sons. Since Mary's family, the Todds, remained in the South, many Northerners never fully trusted their first lady. They believed that she was a Confederate sympathizer, and they often made fun of her eccentricities. Though Lincoln loyally defended Mary, this caused even more tension between the couple.

Lincoln's family life was not always happy; both he and his wife suffered from depression, a debilitating illness that was not well understood or easily treatable at the time. Mary Todd is shown seated at right.

A Night on the Town

On the fateful Friday night—Good Friday, in fact—of the assassination, Mary's mood was much lighter than it had been in a long time. The president, too, was unusually cheerful. Less than a week earlier, General Robert E. Lee had surrendered to General Ulysses S. Grant at Appomattox, Virginia. Earlier, the Emancipation Proclamation had freed more than three million slaves. Peace between the North and South would be uneasy for many years, but Lincoln's generous terms had at least paved the way for tolerance between the two enemy sides. His legacy as president seemed assured.

Ford's Theatre

Ford's Theatre, not far from the White House, was staging *Our American Cousin*, a comedy starring the renowned actress, Laura Keene. The Lincolns attended with Major Henry Rathbone and his fiancée, Miss Clara Harris, the daughter of Senator Ira Harris of New York. The foursome arrived a bit late and were shown to the president's box, which was actually two boxes that had been expanded in honor of the theater's important guests.

The comedy was stopped as the distinguished party entered and the band played "Hail to the Chief" for the president. When the play resumed, audience members noticed that Lincoln and his wife affectionately held hands as they had in their younger days.

The third act had the play's funniest lines, and the audience's attention was fixed on the stage. It was during this time that John Wilkes Booth approached the president's unguarded box. Booth had stopped by Ford's Theatre that morning and had been told that the president would be attending that night's performance. Though Booth was known to be a Confederate sympathizer, no one imagined that he would conspire against the president because of his Southern politics.

The president's security guard, confident that Lincoln was safely enjoying the show in his box, had wandered downstairs to get a better look at the actors. No American president had ever been assassinated, so although the guard's action was later criticized, there was no reason at the time for him to fear foul play. Even if he had remained close to the president, he might never have thought to challenge Booth, who was so well known

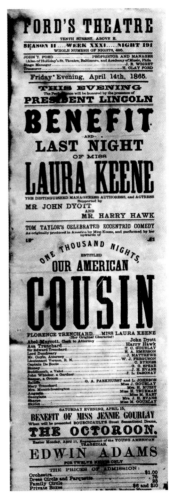

This is an ad for Ford's Theatre, which staged *Our American Cousin* on the night Lincoln was assassinated.

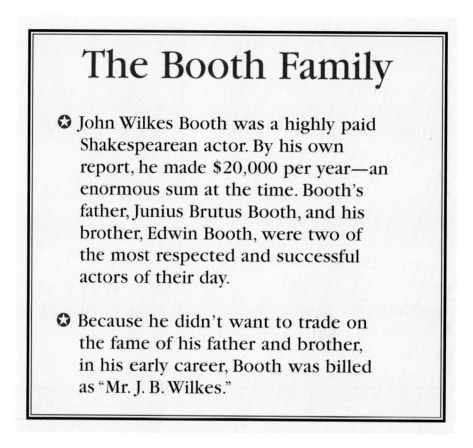

The Booth Family

✪ John Wilkes Booth was a highly paid Shakespearean actor. By his own report, he made $20,000 per year—an enormous sum at the time. Booth's father, Junius Brutus Booth, and his brother, Edwin Booth, were two of the most respected and successful actors of their day.

✪ Because he didn't want to trade on the fame of his father and brother, in his early career, Booth was billed as "Mr. J. B. Wilkes."

to the theater's staff that the ticket taker had waved him through for free that night. To those who noticed Booth, his presence seemed quite ordinary.

The Plot Thickens

Before attending the theater, Booth had had a drink at a nearby tavern in order to quiet his nerves. However, his heart must have been racing as he stealthily cracked open the door of the president's box. Booth had planned out every move in advance. Once inside

This is an artist's depiction of the events at Ford's Theatre on the night that Lincoln was assassinated. Booth snuck into Lincoln's private loge box and took the first family and their guests by surprise.

the box, he bolted the door shut. Armed with a derringer pistol and a dagger, he quickly took aim and fired at the president's head. A ripple of laughter from the audience masked the noise of his shot, but a horrified Major Rathbone saw Lincoln slump forward in his chair. He realized what had happened and lunged at the assassin, who savagely slashed Rathbone in the arm.

The Scene of the Crime

Booth then dramatically leapt from the box, waving his knife and shouting, "Sic semper tyrannis!" (Latin for "thus always with tyrants"). Members of the theater cast and audience also heard him cry, "Freedom!" and

Booth leaps twelve feet from the theater box after shooting President Lincoln.

"The South shall be free!" Booth escaped from Ford's Theatre, but the force of his twelve-foot drop had caused him to break his right leg. This made his getaway much more painful.

Trying to Revive the President

Once the audience understood that the president had been shot, the theater became a mob scene. Terrified men and women shouted and scrambled over each other in their haste to exit. The first surgeon to reach the scene, Dr. Charles A. Leale, performed artificial respiration on Lincoln to try to keep him alive. Dr. Leale recalled that he used two fingers of his right hand to press down the president's paralyzed tongue so that air could enter his lungs. Others moved the patient's long arms to help his chest expand. Laura Keene, the actress, made her way from the stage to the balcony where she gently held Lincoln's wounded head. Before long, his heartbeat revived. As Dr. Leale labored to stabilize the president, he was joined by two others, Dr. Charles Taft and Dr. Albert F. A. King. Dr. Leale knew there was no chance Lincoln would live, for the bullet had torn a path through his brain and was trapped behind an eye. Dr. Leale announced to the others, "His wound is mortal. It is impossible for him to recover."

This photo shows the probe used on Lincoln and two skull fragments that were removed during the autopsy.

It was thought that Lincoln would survive the move to a more suitable place, so the doctors gently lifted him and moved into the crowd. The White House was too far away; the president would surely die before he got there.

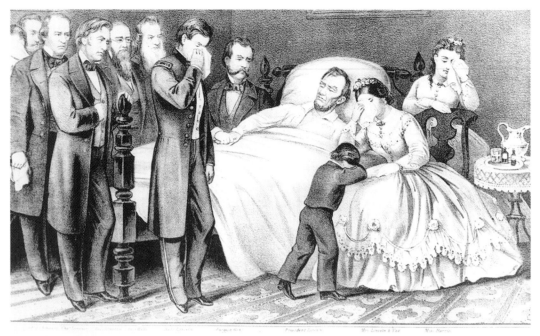

DEATH OF PRESIDENT LINCOLN.
AT WASHINGTON, D. C. APRIL 15TH 1865

This painting is an artist's depiction of Lincoln on his deathbed, surrounded by his family and advisers.

The house across the street from Ford's Theatre, which they tried to enter, was closed, but a man with a lighted candle stood in the door of the Petersen house nearby. He waved the doctors inside, and the unconscious president was gently carried to a small bedroom. Lincoln's progress came to a halt several times so that Dr. Leale could remove blood clots from his head wound.

Lincoln's great height was too much for the small bed. Dr. Leale placed the president on his back and ordered that the end of the bed be removed so that the president's knees would not have to be bent double. When the bed could not be repositioned, Dr. Leale called for extra pillows for Lincoln's head and moved his patient's long body into a diagonal position.

Nearing the End

It soon became clear that Lincoln would not survive. Surgeon General Joseph K. Barnes and Dr. Robert K. Stone, the Lincolns' family doctor, quickly arrived and took charge. They agreed with Dr. Leale that nothing could be done except to keep the patient comfortable, though it seemed unlikely that Lincoln was aware of his surroundings.

Lincoln's eyes, neither of which were responding to light, were black and bruised. The pupil of one eye had shrunk, and the other had grown larger. Blood from the head wound drenched the bed. The president was undressed and mustard plasters—medicinal compresses commonly used in those days—were placed from his neck to his feet, not in an effort to heal him, but in an attempt to warm his cold body and stimulate his nerves.

Another Assassination Attempt

As the long hours passed, the small rooms of the Petersen house became more crowded. Officials arrived with the grim news that Secretary of State William Seward had also been the victim of an assassination attempt—this one a vicious knife attack by an assassin named Lewis Payne, whose real name was Lewis Thorton Powell.

Payne had forced his way into Seward's mansion by claiming to have a delivery of medicine; he knew that Seward was recovering in bed after a carriage accident. Seward's son, Frederick, sensed that something was wrong, but when he tried to keep Payne out, Payne beat him up. Then Payne brutally slashed Seward's throat twice. He would have killed him if Seward had not been wearing a metal neck brace for his injury. Payne fought his way past Seward's other son, Augustus, and a state department visitor, before he ran from the house, confident that Seward would die.

Secretary of State William H. Seward was also the victim of an assassination attempt. He was brutally attacked by Lewis Payne, who left him with a scar from his lip to his chin. Unlike Lincoln, Seward survived.

Rumors spread like wildfire that conspirators wanted to murder Lincoln's entire cabinet, but this turned out to be untrue. When all the facts were sorted out later, however, it seemed that at least some cabinet members and Vice President Andrew Johnson had been targeted.

Good-Bye to Lincoln: A Nation in Mourning

At 6 AM, it began to rain. Mrs. Lincoln and her son, Robert, remained near the president. When he died on April 15 at 7:22 AM, nine hours after Booth had fired his shot, Mrs. Lincoln was inconsolable. According to several people who were also present at Lincoln's bedside, Mary Todd Lincoln wept, "Oh, why didn't he shoot me, too?" Solemn prayers were said over the president's body. Then Edwin M. Stanton, secretary of war, made his famous comment, "Now he is one with the Ages."

By 7:30 AM, bells tolled the sad news all over Washington, D.C., and American flags were lowered to half-staff. Even though rain was pouring, the street outside the Petersen house was packed with a silent, weeping crowd. A procession of bareheaded military officers escorted the president's body back to the White House. As they slowly made their way to the mansion, ordinary citizens who lined the wet pavement removed their hats to show respect. Much was made of the fact that the bad news was transmitted across the nation by telegraph. For one of the first times in American history, people living in the distant states learned the news not much later than those who lived in the capital.

Timeline of Lincoln's Life

February 12, 1809
Lincoln is born in Hardin County, Kentucky.

October 5, 1818
Lincoln's mother, Nancy Hanks Lincoln, dies.

December 2, 1819
His father, Thomas Lincoln, marries his second wife, Sarah Bush Johnston, a widow with three children.

May 7, 1833
Lincoln is named postmaster of New Salem, Illinois.

August 4, 1834
Lincoln is elected to the Illinois Assembly.

August 25, 1835
Lincoln's first love Ann Rutledge dies of "violent fever."

March 1, 1837
Lincoln is formally admitted to the Illinois Bar.

November 4, 1842
Lincoln marries Mary Todd.

August 1, 1843
Robert Todd Lincoln is born.

March 1846
Edward Baker Lincoln is born.

August 3, 1846
Lincoln is elected to the thirtieth U.S. Congress as a Whig.

February 1, 1850
Eddie Lincoln dies.

December 21, 1850
William Wallace Lincoln is born.

January 17, 1851
Lincoln's father, Thomas, dies.

April 4, 1853
Thomas "Tad" Lincoln is born.

1856
Lincoln joins the Republican Party.

November 6, 1860
Lincoln is elected president.

April 12, 1861
Civil War begins when
Confederate states fire
upon Fort Sumter.

February 20, 1862
Willie Lincoln dies.

January 1, 1863
The Emancipation Proclamation
is issued.

November 8, 1864
Lincoln is elected president for a
second term.

April 9, 1865
The Confederate states surrender at
Appomattox, Virginia.

April 14, 1865
John Wilkes Booth fatally shoots
Lincoln at Ford's Theatre.

April 15, 1865
Lincoln dies of gunshot wounds
at the age of fifty-six.

April 19, 1865
Funeral services are held at
the White House.

April 21–May 3, 1865
A funeral train bears Lincoln's body
to its final resting place in
Springfield, Illinois.

May 4, 1865
Lincoln is buried at Oak
Ridge Cemetery.

July 14, 1870
Congress grants Mrs. Lincoln an
annual widow's pension.

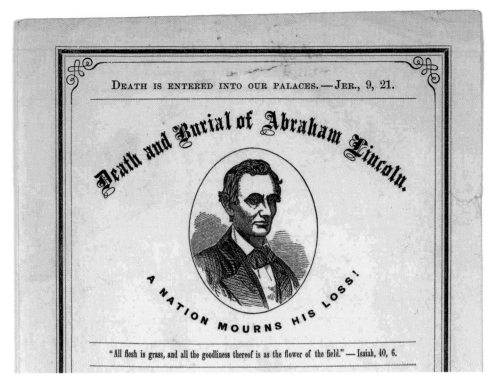

Americans mourned their fallen president in tearful editorials, illustrations, and poems. The tribute above was published in Boston, Massachusetts, just after Lincoln's assassination.

Men and women stopped whatever they were doing to place mourning symbols on houses and public buildings. Newspapers that had, just weeks and months before, viciously criticized the president, now dedicated entire issues to the terrible events. Sorrowful editorials and illustrations paid tribute to Lincoln. It almost seemed as though it took his assassination for the nation to truly appreciate all that Lincoln had done.

Chapter 2

The Climate Surrounding the Assassination

ttacks on President Lincoln had occurred even before the first day of his presidency. In 1860, when he traveled from Illinois for his first inauguration, he was deluged with hate mail and death threats. When news of a plot to murder him in Baltimore was revealed, arrangements were hurriedly changed so that Lincoln could bypass Baltimore and travel ahead to Philadelphia for Washington's birthday ceremonies. Ultimately, Lincoln slipped into Washington, D.C., disguised as a sick passenger aboard a Pullman car—a security measure that backfired when newspapers depicted him as a coward.

Secession and Antislavery: Lincoln's Views

Though the newly elected president promised not to interfere with the slave states' rights, his own antislavery views were widely known and were very

In this painting from 1863, African Americans express their gratitude toward President Lincoln for issuing the Emancipation Proclamation.

threatening to Southerners. He had held these beliefs since boyhood, so everyone understood that he would never permit the spread of slavery beyond its present boundaries. Lincoln also believed that secession—withdrawal from the Union—was illegal and that the Confederates had no right to break away from the rest of the states.

The Civil War

Lincoln was elected president of the entire country, and he took every opportunity to emphasize this during his early days in office. But within weeks of his inauguration, the United States split into two warring camps. The surprise assault on Fort Sumter (Charleston Harbor, South Carolina), triggered the beginning of the bloody Civil War. On April 12, 1861, Confederate troops fired on Union soldiers at Fort Sumter. On April 13, the Union troops surrendered, evacuating the garrison the following day. Although there were no casualties during the attack, two Union soldiers were accidentally killed and two were wounded when a cannon exploded prematurely.

The war raged for four terrible years, dominating virtually every day of Lincoln's presidency. From their first crushing defeat at Bull Run (a Southern base in Virginia) on July 21, 1861, things were tough for the Union. Another bloody defeat for the North followed at Malvern Hill (Poindexter's Farm, Virginia) on July 1, 1862. Union soldiers suffered

This photo of Civil War casualties by famed Civil War photographer Matthew Brady is titled *Incidence of War—A Harvest of Death.*

even greater losses in the second battle of Bull Run and in the battles of Shiloh and Harper's Ferry. In July 1863, General George Meade finally forced a Confederate retreat after a bloody three-day battle at Gettysburg, Pennsylvania. But he stopped short of cutting off General Robert E. Lee's Confederate troops, which enabled them to escape.

The Bloodiest War in American History

Whenever Lincoln knew that a campaign was being waged, he huddled near a telegraph to get the latest news on casualties. More sophisticated weapons were used during the Civil War than in previous conflicts, but soldiers still engaged in old-fashioned hand-to-hand combat on the battlefields, causing body counts to soar to record numbers. Some historians call the Civil War "the first modern war," referring to its sophisticated tactical strategies. But it was also the bloodiest war in American history, leaving few families untouched by death.

The tide finally began to turn for the North in November 1863 when General Ulysses S. Grant drove Confederate troops from Chattanooga, Tennessee. In March 1864, Grant was named commander in chief of the Union forces. It took the fall of Atlanta in 1864 and the fall of Richmond in 1865 to confirm a Union victory.

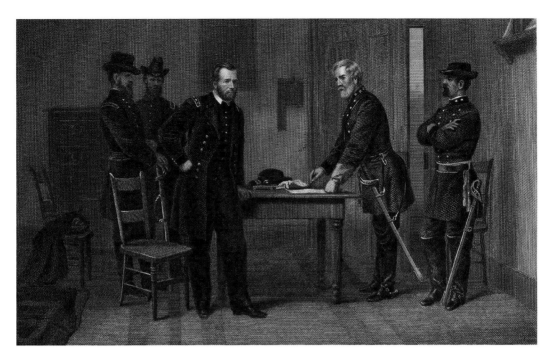

Confederate leader General Robert E. Lee *(with pen in hand)* surrenders to Union leader General Ulysses S. Grant *(leaning on the table)* at the Appomattox Courthouse in Appomattox, Virginia, on April 9, 1865.

The End of the Civil War

When surrender finally came, emotions on both sides—at least among die-hard loyalists—still ran murderously high. General Ulysses S. Grant and General Robert E. Lee behaved with great dignity at the surrender ceremony on April 9, 1865, at Appomattox, Virginia. The terms were generous: Enlisted men would give up their arms, officers would keep theirs, and each man could take a horse or a mule and go home. They would not be troubled by U.S. authorities if they promised not to fight against the Union again. In addition to the basic agreement, Grant took extra food rations from his own soldiers and gave them to the Confederates, who were almost at the point of starvation. When Union soldiers began to fire guns in a victory celebration, Grant made them stop. He reminded his troops that the Confederates were their countrymen again.

Resentment Smolders

This fair treatment should have eased the tensions between the Union and the Confederacy, but few Southerners were ready to forget the bloodshed and the loss of beloved sons, brothers, and fathers. Though the freeing of the slaves was widely celebrated, many Southerners remained angry that it forcibly changed their way of life and rendered their plantations inoperable. Although the vast majority of Americans accepted the terms of surrender, isolated Confederate loyalists could not bring themselves to accept them, no matter how well their compatriots were treated. This was the climate that swirled around John Wilkes Booth and his friends as they hatched their plot against President Abraham Lincoln.

John Wilkes Booth and the Unfolding of the Assassination

John Wilkes Booth was a famous and acclaimed actor, a member of one of the most highly regarded theatrical families in America. In 1865, his murder of Lincoln was as astonishing to the public as if a top film star were arrested for assassinating a president today.

John Wilkes Booth

Because of Booth's remarkable career and rare success, his planning of the Lincoln conspiracy remains a particular mystery. Why would a man who enjoyed fame, good fortune, creative work, a loving family, and a circle of stimulating friends throw it all away to become the most hated criminal of his day?

Portrait of a Killer

Most assassins are underachievers, misfits, and loners. However, Booth was just the opposite: a handsome, outgoing man who easily attracted friendship. Most men gladly would have exchanged places with him.

This photograph of assassin John Wilkes Booth was taken in the early 1860s.

Yet something in his nature was dark and brooding. He also had a small but troublesome secret in his past: His father, Junius, had run away from an early marriage in England, and John Wilkes himself was the product of Junius's second, common-law marriage to Mary Ann Holmes. The couple fled to America and kept details of their union quiet. Junius's common-law marriage had not kept him from achieving prominence in the American theater, but it probably gave the Booth family a sense of living just outside the fringes of polite society.

Obsessed with the Confederate Cause

John Wilkes Booth was often described as excitable, with intense highs and lows. But it was his obsession with the Confederate cause, not his temperament, that cemented his desire to kill the president.

Though Northerners believed in the unification of the two sides, and most Southerners accepted their defeat and the need for reconstruction, Booth stubbornly held on to the belief that the South's principles were in the right, that the Confederacy could yet come out the winner. Booth was pro-slavery, admired the Southern code of chivalry and its aristocratic lifestyle, and believed that Southern traditions should be allowed to go on. Finally, the way the war was conducted at its close outraged him. His resentment of Lincoln and the Union reached its peak when, in the final days of battle, exchanges of prisoners were frozen. Booth mistakenly believed that if he kidnapped the president, Confederate

Assassination Facts

☼ Lincoln was the first U.S. president to be assassinated.

☼ Though it has never been proven, Lincoln's appearance (while alive) has led scientists to ask if he suffered from Marfan's syndrome, a condition that can lead to fatal heart and blood vessel defects. Some think that if the president had not been murdered, he would have died from the effects of Marfan's before the end of 1865.

☼ General and Mrs. Ulysses S. Grant were supposed to go to Ford's Theatre with the Lincolns that fateful night, but Mary Lincoln had once insulted Julia Grant in front of a group of military officers. Afterward, Mrs. Grant disliked the first lady so much that she refused to socialize with her. Staying away from Ford's Theatre because of the ladies' feud probably saved General Grant's life.

☼ Lincoln received only a spoonful of diluted brandy after the assassination. No other medicine was used.

☼ Some fifty-five people visited Lincoln before he died (though not all at the same time).

☼ Though he was a lawyer and understood the importance of making his will, Lincoln died without one.

☼ An autopsy was performed by physicians of the Army Medical Museum (now known as the Armed Forces

Institute of Pathology). Results were quickly released to the public to quash rumors about the president's death.

✪ The $100,000 reward offered by the U.S. War Department was meant to speed up the capture of Lincoln's assassin and coconspirators. Instead, it resulted in a large number of private detectives withholding information. They hoped to lay sole claim to the prize and refused to share any of the clues they had unearthed.

✪ Lincoln's handsome mahogany coffin was six feet six inches in length and one and a half feet wide.

✪ Lincoln's body was accompanied on the funeral train by the casket of Willie Lincoln. The little boy had been disinterred so that father and son could be buried next to each other in their home state of Illinois.

✪ Mary Lincoln did not attend her husband's funeral. She was reported to be distraught, but she may have been afraid to mingle with those she considered her enemies.

✪ In 1865, hundreds of clergymen threw out their Easter sermons and instead spoke about the tragedy and the symbolism of Lincoln's Good Friday assassination.

✪ Lincoln's body was buried and reburied for security reasons. His casket was then encased in cement and buried a final time. On that occasion, a group of local citizens peered in at the corpse to confirm that it was Lincoln's.

and Union prisoners could once again be exchanged. Once Booth had successfully captured Lincoln, he felt that Americans would rally to support him. Somehow Booth convinced himself that this criminal act would make him a national hero.

Booth's Initial Plan

Few recall that Booth's original idea was not to kill the president, but to capture him alive and trade him for Confederate prisoners of war. This would have been hard to pull off, as the president could have been way-laid as he traveled. Booth and his fellow conspirators agreed on the deed and the time of the kidnapping: March 17, 1865, as the president traveled to the Soldiers' Home. Ultimately, Lincoln failed to make his trip, so the kidnapping plan was a failure. Soon after, the surrender at Appomattox and the release of all pris-oners of war made another kidnapping try uncalled for. Booth, described as "restless and bitter" in the days fol-lowing the war's end, at last decided that Lincoln and at least some members of his cabinet had to be murdered.

A Hunted Man

One of the saddest entries in Booth's journal was made after the assassination, when in his last days, in pain from the break in his right leg that he suffered after his wild leap to the stage of Ford's Theatre, he began to grasp that he had made a terrible error in judgment. Booth had become the most hated man in the Union, hunted on every side. His famous face made it certain that he would be recognized and captured; there could be no escape. Instead of rejoicing at a tyrant's death, like Booth had believed they would, the American people plunged into deep mourning for President Lincoln, and praised him as a great man.

Second Thoughts

Desperate and confused, Booth began to wonder how God would judge him. When planning the

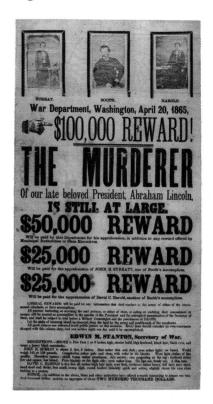

A fortune was offered to anyone who could catch the conspirators. Thousands of citizens joined in the search for Lincoln's killer and his accomplices.

assassination, he was certain that the death of the president would serve the highest good of the nation. Confronted with heartfelt newspaper tributes to Lincoln that were smuggled to him in his hiding place, Booth ached at the thought of the trouble he had given his family. Imagining his mother's sorrow gave him special regret. Booth understood that he would die on the run, probably soon, and only hoped that he could die bravely, rather than like a hunted animal.

The Telltale Diary

As lawmen were closing in on him, Booth recorded his thoughts in his diary. It is because of this that modern historians know exactly what was going on in his mind. Though Booth felt very much alone, he hadn't been: As the actor polished his plans to kill Lincoln, he received needed support from others. He sought out like-minded helpers, people who loved the South and were unafraid of personal danger.

Booth's Loyal Followers

To assemble the most loyal and capable team he could, Booth turned first to friends he had grown up with and trusted for years—men who felt, as he did, that the Confederacy had been terribly wronged. Most histories of the day make a point that the actor, who had plenty of money, used all of his charms and resources to encourage these people to give him assistance.

Samuel Arnold, a farmhand from Hookstown, Maryland, had attended St. Timothy's Hall in Cantonsville, Maryland, with Booth when both were boys. Arnold was charged with counseling, combining, and confederating with the other conspirators.

Michael O'Laughlen also was a school friend of Booth's. He worked in a livery stable and had an alcohol problem. He was charged with lying in wait

Led by John Wilkes Booth, this group allegedly planned and carried out the assassination of President Abraham Lincoln on April 14, 1865. Four of the accused conspirators, Mary Surratt, Lewis Payne, David Herold, and George Atzerodt, were convicted and hanged.

to murder General Ulysses S. Grant, who had inadvertently saved his own life by deciding not to join the Lincolns at the theater.

Edman "Ned" Spangler was a stage carpenter at Ford's Theatre and an avid Potomac crab fisherman. He curried Booth's horse and slept in a stable behind the theater. Some people believe that Spangler kept people away from the presidential box while Booth was murdering President Lincoln.

John Surratt (Mary Surratt's son), was a clerk for the Adams Express Company when he befriended John Wilkes Booth. Surratt also had served as a Confederate spy. Once Wilkes pulled him into the conspiracy, Surratt quit his clerkship to focus on the plot full-time.

George Atzerodt was a poor carriage maker who had also assisted Confederate spies during the war. He was considered an expert on the Maryland back roads. In addition to helping plan Booth's escape, he was charged with lying in wait with intent to murder Vice President Andrew Johnson in his rooms at the Kirkwood Hotel. Atzerodt and Booth had a fight when, at the last minute, Atzerodt argued that he had agreed to kidnapping, and not to murder.

Lewis Thorton Powell, also known as Lewis Payne, or Lewis Paine, was a Confederate recruit from

Conspiracy Facts

✪ The gun that Booth used to assassinate Lincoln was a single-shot muzzle-loading Philadelphia derringer with a percussion cap. It shot a round lead ball.

✪ Booth's fellow conspirators were tried by a military court just as the U.S. Supreme Court was getting ready to rule that no civilian should be tried by the military if a civilian court was available. Had this ruling come down just a little earlier, it could have saved the lives of the four conspirators who were eventually executed. David Herold was ultimately charged with aiding and assisting Booth to escape, and for harboring the knowledge that Booth had assassinated the president.

Florida who bitterly hated the Union. The son of a Baptist minister and a born-again Christian, Payne nevertheless fought from the time he was sixteen until he was twenty. The charges against him were assaulting, cutting, and wounding Secretary Seward with the intent to murder him. He came very close to succeeding; the gash on Seward's face cut deeply into his jaw. Of all the conspirators, Payne was considered the most deadly, after Booth.

Mary Surratt (John Surratt's mother) owned a boarding house at 541 H Street. Earlier, she had run a tavern named Surrattsville that also served as a polling place and post office; with money scarce, she rented the place to an ex-policeman named John Lloyd and turned to the respectable job of providing bed and board for paying guests. Mrs. Surratt greatly enjoyed the dashing company of John Wilkes Booth, whom she met through her son, John. The other conspirators often visited 541 H Street; evidence suggests that the Surratt establishment was a safe house for Confederate sympathizers during the war. A Roman Catholic convert and the only woman charged, Mary Surratt was accused of harboring, concealing, counseling, aiding, and abetting all the defendants.

Dr. Samuel A. Mudd gave Booth a night's shelter after he had assassinated the president. He also set Booth's leg, carefully cutting off his distinctive leather boot in the process.

David Herold: Booth's Most Loyal Follower

A man named David Herold was the one supporter who accompanied Booth to the bitter end. Herold, the only son of a widowed mother and the brother of seven sisters, was reputed to be "simpleminded."

Booth and Herold were found hiding in a tobacco barn near Bowling Green, Virginia. When manhunters tried to flush them out, Herold surrendered, but Booth refused to come out and was shot.

However, he knew the back roads of Maryland and was able to help Booth find food and shelter. He also helped Booth get around since his broken leg caused him tremendous pain and he could not walk on it.

Game Over

Eleven days after Lincoln was assassinated, on April 26, 1865, Lieutenant Col. Everett J. Conger, who led the manhunt, finally tracked Booth and Herold down. They were hiding near Bowling Green, Virginia, in the tobacco barn of a farmer named Richard Garrett. Garrett was ordered to go into the barn and give the two fugitives the order to surrender. When he returned, he reported that Booth had threatened to shoot him.

A shouting match between the lawmen and the two fugitives then broke out. Booth yelled that they had better prepare a stretcher for him if they planned to take him; they would not capture him alive. He bargained for a chance to try escaping, but Lt. Conger would have none of it. Tired and scared out of his wits, David Herold finally decided to give himself up. Booth was furious, but Herold left the barn with his hands in the air.

Finally, they tried to smoke Booth out of the barn. A fire was set to some hay inside the building. Sergeant Boston Corbett, acting without orders, took advantage of the moment of confusion and shot Booth through a crack in the barn, fatally wounding him. Lieutenant Luther Baker went to Booth's aid, gently supporting his head while Lt. Conger inspected his wound. The stricken Booth was moved to a straw-stuffed mattress on the front porch of the Garrett house. He said, "Tell Mother I died for my country." He then asked to be turned over on his face. Soon afterward, he died.

The Reaction to Lincoln's Assassination

After Lincoln's death, all government and private offices and businesses in Washington D.C., closed. The president's body was embalmed and his open casket was placed in a position of honor in the East Room of the White House. On April 17, 1865, the doors were thrown open to the public. Some 25,000 people waited patiently for as long as six hours to glimpse their president's face for the last time. The room was filled with white flowers and the walls were draped with black cloth. Soldiers with drawn muskets served as an honor guard, letting visitors in just a few at a time. The splendid mahogany casket had four immense decorative handles on each side and heavy gold fringe that hung from the top. A large silver emblem gave the sixteenth president's name along with the dates of his birth and death.

Lincoln's Final Journey

Five thousand military officers of every rank marched in the funeral cortege. George Alfred Townsend, correspondent for the *New York World*, reported that thirty bands participated in the procession. All of them played mournful songs. Heavy military artillery, brightly polished for the occasion, rolled along behind. Townsend wrote that it was a strange occasion because although it was the grandest parade in anyone's memory, it was also by far the saddest. A feeling of oppression settled over Washington. At 3 PM, Lincoln's casket was transported to the Capitol for the last time, where more members of the public were allowed to pay their respects.

Finally, on April 21, 1865, the president's body was conveyed to the train depot, where his private car—built in military workshops for the president's exclusive use during his lifetime—was waiting for the 1,700-mile trip to Springfield, Illinois. The car had twelve windows on each side, luxurious mahogany paneling, and a Brussels carpet. Now it served as his hearse.

The Funeral Train

Major General E. D. Townsend was in charge of the funeral train, which consisted of eight cars in addition to the one that carried the president. These eight were specially furnished by the eight companies that owned the rail rights to Springfield. Major General Townsend wrote that hundreds of thousands of men, women, and

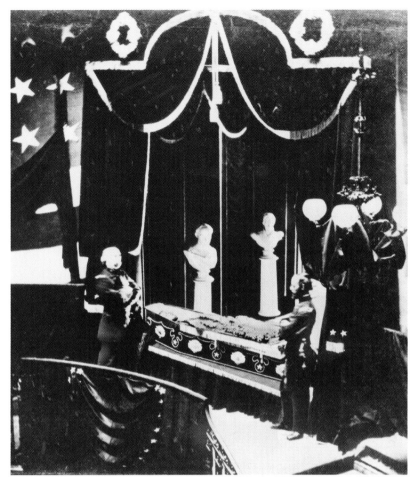

This is the only photo of President Lincoln's body lying in state for a public viewing at city hall in New York. Out of respect for the president, no other photos were permitted.

children stood silently or knelt in prayer as the train carrying the president passed. Stops were made in Baltimore, Harrisburg, Philadelphia, New York, Albany, Buffalo, Cleveland, Columbus, Indianapolis, and Chicago. Then came the final stop at Springfield, where the state house and Lincoln's home had been draped in black. Local citizens had worked for two days to prepare the site and assemble a choir of 250 voices to sing "Peace, Troubled Soul" at the burial ceremony.

The president's final journey home was completed just a little more than six weeks after he had delivered his second inaugural address.

Lincoln's Widow

While the country honored Lincoln's memory, his widow, Mary, remained in solitude. Never emotionally strong, she could not or would not participate in the state funeral. Her grief was raw and frantic. In addition to her heartache, she was desperately frightened by the thought of a future without her husband. Deeply in debt, with few friends and a host of real and imagined enemies, Mary became despondent and would not leave her bed. In the days following Lincoln's death, some people who saw Mary wrote that she spoke calmly; others wrote that she was in hysterics. Both accounts were probably true, as Mary dissolved in tears whenever she saw a new visitor but she had quiet periods in between.

President Lincoln's Final Resting Spot

Mary's decision about the site for Lincoln's burial angered the people of Springfield, Illinois. Citizens of Lincoln's hometown had made elaborate arrangements to receive the president's body, but his widow insisted that it be transported to Chicago. Then she changed her mind and agreed that it could be buried in Springfield—but in Oak Ridge Cemetery instead of the idyllic setting the townspeople had bought and prepared. Her insistence was widely resented as insensitive; her wishes were honored, but only for the time being. Later, Lincoln's body would be transferred to its permanent site at Oak Ridge Cemetery.

Mary's Unhappy Future

Mary Lincoln's fears about her own future came to pass. At one point, her son Robert committed her to an asylum for the mentally ill. In her last days, she moved in with her sister, Mrs. Elizabeth Ninian W. Edwards, who, with her husband, occupied the Springfield home where Mary had lived, courted, and married Lincoln. As the president's widow, she was granted an annual Congressional pension of $3,000, plus an outright grant of $15,000. Lincoln's family were legal claimants to his estate, meaning that they inherited what had been his—an estate valued at more than $100,000. In the 1800s, this would have kept most widows in great comfort for the rest of their lives, but Mary's compulsive spending and her breakdowns kept her on the brink of bankruptcy.

After the Death of Booth

After John Wilkes Booth died, Lieutenant Col. Everett J. Conger took the assassin's pistol and carbine (a short-barreled, lightweight firearm originally used by cavalry), diary, and other personal possessions and set out for Washington, D.C., leaving Lieutenant Luther Baker to transport Booth's body in an old market wagon to the Belle Plain landing, where it was loaded onto the deck of the *John S. Ide*. It was later transferred to a government tugboat and finally taken aboard the monitor (war ship) *Montauk* on Thursday, April 27, at 1:45 AM.

Once on board, an autopsy was performed by Dr. Joseph K. Barnes and Dr. Joseph J. Woodward. The doctors determined that as a result of his wounds, Booth likely died of asphyxia about two hours after he was shot. Later, the body was loaded into a rowboat, as though officers were planning to sink it in the Potomac River. Instead, they waited until dark and then, on the orders of Secretary of War Stanton, they secretly moved it for burial to the Old Penitentiary on the Washington Arsenal grounds. There, the body was placed in a simple wood coffin and buried under the floor of the cell.

Booth's Final Resting Spot

In 1867, Booth's body was exhumed and reburied in a locked storeroom of Warehouse 1 of the prison. On June 26, 1869, his body was exhumed and buried again, this time in the family plot in Green Mount Cemetery in Baltimore, Maryland. At the request of the Booth family, the grave remains unmarked to this day.

How Lincoln's Assassination Changed the Course of History

Because Abraham Lincoln was assassinated just days after his second inauguration, the country was robbed of his experienced leadership during the difficult first years of Reconstruction, when the United States was directly governing the defeated Southern states. Many people believe that Lincoln's death ended all hope of "magnanimous leadership"— meaning the prospect of peace and teamwork between the victorious North and the defeated South.

This is probably true, for though Lincoln got off to a shaky start in his first term, by 1865 he enjoyed a position of strength. General Grant's victories gave him the peace he wanted, as well as a second term in the White House. Lincoln vowed to treat defeated Southerners kindly, not only for reasons of state, but also because his own in-laws were among the defeated. General Robert E. Lee's gratitude for the fair treatment of his soldiers at Appomattox was a clear signal that most Southerners were ready to put ill will behind them. With Lincoln at the helm, and General Lee setting the Southern tone, reunification would have proceeded much more smoothly.

Old Wounds Reopened

Unfortunately, Lincoln's murder by a Southern loyalist reopened many old wounds, making it harder for the North and South to become partners after the war. The Military Commission trial of those who conspired against Lincoln also angered many Southern sympathizers. The trial was held in the Old Arsenal, Quarters 20, on what is now Washington, D.C.'s Fort Lesley J. McNair. It lasted for almost all of May and June 1865, and was a continuing spectacle of Union military men harshly judging shackled Southern loyalists.

The Ultimate Penalty

On July 7, 1865, George Atzerodt, David Herold, Lewis Payne, and Mary Surratt were hanged for their crimes at the Old Penitentiary. Mary Surratt was widowed, hard working, gentle, and devoutly religious, and her execution—in a time when women were almost never brought to the gallows—caused a great deal of public outrage.

In the years that followed, Southerners and the Union victors engaged in bloody fights and lingering resentment. Though the slaves were free, their lives, too, were harder than anyone had predicted. The Ku Klux Klan was founded during Reconstruction. Years of lynching and terror began. The war was over, but it took many years for real, healing peace to take root in the South.

George Atzerodt, David Herold, Lewis Payne, and Mary Surratt were publicly hanged at the Old Penitentiary for their respective roles in the plot to assassinate President Lincoln.

What Happened to the Remaining Conspirators?

✪ Samuel Arnold and Michael O'Laughlen were each sentenced to life in prison. Dr. Samuel A. Mudd, too, was sentenced to life, but to this day, his descendants work in the courts to prove his innocence. Edman Spangler was sentenced to just six years in prison.

✪ John Surratt, son of the condemned Mary Surratt, escaped capture for a time by traveling to Europe and enlisting in the army of Pope Pius the ninth. Discovered in Italy, he made his way to Egypt, but he was sent back to the United States to face justice. In 1867, his trial ended with a hung jury, meaning that the jurors couldn't reach an agreement. The government freed him on bail pending another trial, but they never prosecuted him again.

Historians continue to believe that if Lincoln had not been assassinated, much of the bitterness and bloodshed of the years following 1865 could have been avoided. Lincoln was not a perfect president or a flawless man, but his deep sense of fairness and his great heart would have served the country well during the first four postwar years.

This is the flag that decorated the presidential box at Ford's Theatre the night of Abraham Lincoln's assassination. It is displayed at the Connecticut Historical Society in Hartford, Connecticut. Period illustrations suggest that the president might have clutched the flag after he was shot by John Wilkes Booth.

The Martyr

The way Lincoln died is an important part of his legend. He was the first U.S. president ever to be assassinated. Americans considered him a martyr to the cause of freedom, and that is how he is still remembered. He died at the highest point of his lifework, when peace was newly won and soldiers were free to make their way home to waiting families. His loss to the country was profound and terrible; but in terms of his myth, he could not have chosen better than to end his work at its greatest moment, on a threshold of bright promise, when all knew he had done well.

Historic Timeline

1830s–1865

The underground railroad—the effort to assist runaway slaves in bondage in the North to escape from slavery—is in operation.

1831

Slave Nat Turner leads the only black rebellion in U.S. history against slavery; more than fifty whites are killed before the rebellion is quashed.

1852

Harriet Beecher Stowe writes *Uncle Tom's Cabin*, an antislavery novel.

1857

The U.S. Supreme Court, in *Scott v. Sanford* (also known as the Dred Scott decision), legalizes slavery in U.S. territories and declares the Missouri Compromise of 1820-1821 unconstitutional.

1859

Harper's Ferry raid, an unsuccessful attempt by John Brown to start a slave uprising.

1860

South Carolina votes to secede from the Union following election of Abraham Lincoln to presidency.

1861

The Confederacy is established at the Montgomery Convention; Jefferson Davis becomes Confederate president.

The American Civil War begins; it is fought from 1861 to 1865.

1863

The Emancipation Proclamation technically frees slaves in Confederate-held territories.

1865

General Robert E. Lee surrenders at Appomattox Courthouse.

The Thirteenth Amendment, which prohibits slavery, is ratified.

Lincoln is shot and killed at Ford's Theatre in Washington, D.C.

The Battle of Gettysburg is fought; Confederate charges fail to dislodge Union troops, which becomes a turning point of the war.

Glossary

Appomattox Virginia village where General Robert E. Lee surrendered the Confederate armies to General Ulysses S. Grant and his Union troops on April 9, 1865.

aristocracy Privileged ruling class, such as the planners of the Confederacy.

artificial respiration Medical act to help a patient's breathing.

asphyxia Death resulting from lack of oxygen.

box Private space usually held for important members of an audience in a theater.

chivalry Qualities such as courage and the protection of women that were much idealized by Confederate troops and Southerners.

conspiracy Agreement to commit a crime.

contempt Scorn.

cortege Funeral parade.

derringer Short-barreled pistol of the sort used in Lincoln's assassination.

disinterred Unburied; removed from original grave site.

emancipate Free; the Emancipation Proclamation was the document that freed the slaves.

hearse Vehicle that carries a dead body.

invalid Sick person.

livery   Care and boarding of horses for a fee.

mahogany   Rich wood from which Lincoln's casket was made.

mortal   Having to do with death.

mustard plaster   Warmed healing compress used to comfort ailing parts of the body and to stimulate the nerves.

pension   Sum of money usually paid for years of service in the workforce, but in Mary Todd Lincoln's case, it was paid by the government for her service as first lady.

prosecute   To take legal action against.

Reconstruction   Period from 1865 to 1877 during which the Union controlled the states of the defeated Confederacy before they were readmitted to the United States.

séance   Meeting at which persons attempt to receive spiritual messages.

siege   Blockade of a town or fortress by any army determined to capture it.

surgeon general   Most senior doctor in the U.S. government.

sympathizer   Someone who supports a cause; John Wilkes Booth was a Confederate sympathizer.

telegraph   Communications system that transmitted and received electrical impulses that could be decoded; a state-of-the-art method for sharing news during the Civil War.

unification   Joining together, as of the Confederacy and the Union.

For More Information

Abraham Lincoln Online: Assassination and Memorial Links

The following resources and links offer fascinating insight into the life and death of Abraham Lincoln, America's sixteenth president.

A Brief Description of John Wilkes Booth's Family
http://www.surratt.org/su_jwb.html

The Death of John Wilkes Booth, 1865
http://www.ibiscom.com/booth.htm

Ford's Theatre National Historic Site
http://www.nps.gov/foth/bullet.htm

John Wilkes Booth's Autopsy Site
http://home.att.net/~rjnorton/Lincoln83.html

Surratt House Museum Web Site
http://www.surratt.org

Virtual Library: Assassination of President Abraham Lincoln/Library of Congress
http://lcweb2.loc.gov/ammem/alhtml/alrintr.html

The Web of Conspiracy: Reports and Coverage of the Lincoln Conspiracy Trial
http://members.aol.com/historn/index.htm

White House Funeral Sermon for President Lincoln
http://showcase.netins.net/web/creative/lincoln/speeches/gurley.htm

Documentary

American Experience: Abraham and Mary Lincoln: A House Divided, David Grubin Productions, Inc. (Video). Available from PBS Home Video.

For Further Reading

Bishop, Jim. *The Day Lincoln Was Shot.* New York: Outlet, 1997.

Booth, John Wilkes. *Right or Wrong, God Judge Me: The Writings of John Wilkes Booth.* Edited by Louise Taper and John Rhodehamel. Urbana, IL: University of Illinois Press, 1997.

Good, Timothy S., ed. *We Saw Lincoln Shot: One Hundred Eyewitness Accounts.* Jackson, MS: University Press of Mississippi, 1995.

Ownsbey, Betty J. *Alias "Paine": Lewis Thornton Powell, the Mystery Man of the Lincoln Conspiracy.* Jefferson, NC: McFarland & Company, 1993.

Steers, Edward, Jr. *His Name Is Still Mudd: The Case Against Doctor Samuel Alexander Mudd.* Gettysburg, PA: Thomas Publications, 1997.

Trindal, Elizabeth Steger. *Mary Surratt: An American Tragedy.* Gretna, LA: Pelican Publishing Company, 1996.

Zeinert, Karen. *The Lincoln Murder Plot.* North Haven, CT: Linnet Books, 1999.

Index

About the Author

Deborah A. Marinelli holds a Ph.D. in English from the State University of New York at Albany and an M.A. in liberal arts education from St. John's College, Santa Fe, New Mexico. A professional writer, researcher, and editor for twenty years, she has published fiction and nonfiction with Scholastic Books, Playboy Press, and Houghton Mifflin, among others. She also teaches writing in Troy, New York.

Photo Credits

Cover photo © Corbis; p. 1 © Medford Historical Society Collection/Corbis; p. 4 © James P. Blair/Corbis; p. 6 © David J. & Janice L. Frent Collection/Corbis; pp. 7, 9, 11, 13, 15, 16, 26, 29, 39, 43, 47, 53 © Bettmann/Corbis; p. 17 © Historical Collections, National Museum of Health and Medicine, AFIP; p. 18 © Culver Pictures; p. 20 Courtesy of Seward House, Auburn, NY; pp. 24, 27, 37 © Library of Congress, Prints & Photographs Division; p. 32 © Hulton/Archive; p. 55 © AP/Wide World Photo.

Series Design and Layout

Les Kanturek